THE MOST WANTED GIRLS
MASONIA WILLIAMS

The Most Wanted Girls

The Most Wanted, Volume 1

Masonia Williams

Published by Masonia Williams, 2023.

THE MOST WANTED GIRLS

First edition. September 14, 2023.

ISBN: 979-8223752981

Written by Masonia Williams.

THE MOST WANTED GIRLS

Chapter I

KANSAS JUVENILE CORRECTION COMPLEX
Flashback (2032)

Chains rattle as the inmates walk. Officers direct them to their cells. Standing in a straight line each officer waited for each inmate's cell to open. Urella Keirl staring at the empty bunk on top of her. Being calmly observing. She eyed the new inmate as the face couldn't be seen. It was like a shadow of their bodies. Urella glanced back at the bunk ceiling. Mela standing in one place, not sure what to do next. Glancing at her surroundings. The officer slowly took the chains off her ankles.

Mela sighs as she was in the middle of her meditation. Going back into it. She dreamed of a more fairytale dream.

A long ruffle dress drags the floor, crossing over a dead body on the black ebony stairs. Heels clack the floor, tilted light bug dozes off as soon as the mistress walks up the last of the stairs, picking up her dress, glancing down to watch her step. The second light blackouts once she looked over her shoulder gracefully. Walking forward in the hallway once she stepped up the last step. Taking off her heels walking, non-stopping taking off her gown, running to a no exist hallway.

A white Mustang pulls up. The bare footed princess jogs down the stairs, running to her lover with free arms, leaning over for a kiss. They get in the car, the tires revs. The girl cheers as she excitedly closes her eyes for the moment. Slowly pulling out her blade. While the driver has no clue of what may happen next.

Mela wakes up to the dream but was it a dream? She panicked as she saw the blood on her shirt. Was it hers? Was it her lover? walks up to the sink, rushing trying to get the blood out. Everything she needed was in that sink. All she needed was to stay calm and understand what was at stake. Was she wearing gloves?

Stopping in the middle of her tracks. She stares at herself deadly in the mirror, speaks to herself calmly but doesn't answer herself. "What have you done? " Can you remember anything?" The door knocks and she is out of that dream in two seconds.

A 5 year old news paper was on Mela's desk. Reading about herself was an absolute bomb. Knowing how society still talks.

In Bold letters it reads

11-YEAR-OLD MELA JUNEAU DOES 5 YEARS FOR PREMEDITATED MURDER.

The next segment article reads

COMMISSIONER SKY JUNEAU AND MAE JUNEAU FACE BACKLASH FOR DAUGHTERS DESTRUCTIVE BEHAVIOR.

Stating how poor of a daughter they raised and how my dad worked after voting him out of being commissioner.

The pencil rolls over on the desk, and hits the floor as it continues to roll. Phone buzzes. Not once but twice as it continues. As the girl scrolls through her Instagram, ignoring the call that says "Mom". She finally answers.

"Hello?" She spoke

Her mom sighs as she gathers her thoughts to hear what she has to say. Another drastically sighs comes.

"Mom, what is it?" She asked.

Mela, you are going to go live with your uncle for a few days. Her mother said.

And when you say a few days, what does that inquire? Mela asked

Maybe until you get into college? And then you're on your own from there. Your father thinks it's a great idea for you to learn independence, adulthood, responsibilities- Click.

Mela hung up the phone before her mother got a word in. Since she was at home by herself, she packed her bags, took only what she needed.

The rest was rented. The Computer was the first thing she spot without hesitation, along with her phone, and her most expensive sketchbooks. The car rented but paid in full since she was a straight A student. Her savings were hers, but her parents had control of what she could have. And the list goes on.

Before heading out the door, she took one last look at the family pictures on the wall before she went barging into her father's and mother's room to find her car keys. Although the code on the door was difficult. There was a code in each room.

Fuck that she thought. She went to go get a chainsaw and sliced through that door without alarming anything.

She glanced through drawers to find it. Finally, she found it. It was right between paper stickers and pencil holder. The keys to her hummer that she wanted all year long. Mela glanced out the window to see if her parents were going to show up without announcing but she had plenty of time to make her getaway.

The garage door opened, and the hummer took off. As soon as she took off, her parents were arriving. Her parents looked confused but didn't know anything different at all. She was gone.

No letter, no warning.

Her father searched around the house for Mela but couldn't find her. The money that he had in his safe was gone, along with his checkbooks. Credit cards but he didn't check to see if anything was taken.

2hrs later Mela approached a nice home in a lovely neighborhood. Where there was peace, not a lot of drama per say. The car light turned off as soon as she drove to the corner looking at her boyfriend's house.

As if she was expecting to murder or to catch him cheating. Another Chrysler was parked in Arson driveway. Mela didn't want to assume, so she called again. Busy ring tone.

A young lady with nice hair, perky boobs, toned legs, walked out of Arsons house. Hair blew in the girl's face, and it was hard to get a nice look at her. Praying to see what she looks like and why he chose her. Mela gasps in surprise. Although she didn't cry. The two happy couples kissed before they went inside. Arson gave a look back across the street as if he knew Mela was watching.

The anger she felt was straight piercing, shot in the chest, something that you can't erase or heal from. A scar left provoked.

Mela drove fast towards his car, bumping the back of his new Ford Truck. By the time he ran out to see what went down. She was gone.

In panic, he called the police. The police didn't come until a couple minutes later.

COLORADO

Mela arrived in Colorado on an almost empty tank of gas. She pulled up to an empty gas station. Two cars sped off. Mela looked at the cars drive away as if the police were chasing them.

"Hello?" She spoke. Walking into a ghost town store, full of drinks, smoke, and all above. Another person came in, out of breath. Grabbing random cigarettes. Mela nodded as she walked a little further into the store.

She walked to the back, bathroom to the right. A door says Employees only, cracked to peak in. The clerk fucking someone. Mela gave a bitter smile. Moaning continues. Mela walked behind the counter, took most of the money out. Back and forth she went in emptying out shelves of food. That she could carry out. The only that she forgot was that there were cameras that were being monitored 24/7 by officers.

Although she came in bluntly. No purge mask, nothing. Her stupidity was the only thing that got the best of her. Something she didn't think that she needed help with. She took too long to notice anything.

The next state she pulled up in was deserted. Outside was mountains. A little cafe restaurant was stuck in the middle of nowhere and a drug store was across the way. Like a country dessert. Mela looked young and small like a toothpick. L.A Color lip gloss she pulls out, unscrewing the top, placing the lip cushion on her lips. Lip gloss spread over her lips nicely and slowly. Wigs in her gym bag along with clothes, money, guns and chains. An elder man watched her closely but didn't approach.

Newspaper 50 cents it said on the stand. Mela puts the cents in the man's hands. The man nods but follows her.

TEXAS

Police arrive, they knock, Mae opens the door to let the police in. Mr. And Mrs. Juneau., may we come in? Yes, Mr. Juneau said.

They sat in the living room, drinking tea, Mae served the officer tea, but the officer refused.

How long has your daughter been gone? About a couple of hours. The mother said

A couple of days. The father interrupted.

She was- the officer intercepting the father. The father gave a look at the officer without speaking.

I'm sorry, sir. Please continue.

The father sips his tea before speaking.

Mela, my daughter, was supposed to go to her uncle's house to go to Harvard. Her tuition was fully paid, no students loans, all out of pocket. We saved that money for her to Princeton, Harvard or Yale.

There is no law broken here. If she felt the need to leave or felt unsafe or forced to leave the comfort of her own home. Then she has every right to leave. And go somewhere safe.

"I don't want to hear that shit. You find my daughter and I mean quickly. "The mother said sternly.

The officers nod, leaving silently.

She has all the tools, Mae. Speaking to herself. We taught her how to con, steal, observe the weak and ace the unfortunate and be good at what she does without hesitation. Mae, she will be okay. "The father said

Sky, What if she con's us? Her own flesh and blood? The ones that taught her how to survive amongst wolves in sheep clothing.

Coaches don't teach their students everything and by surprise. If she does. She will regret it.

Sky, we taught her too well for 16 years. She knows too much. The mother says worried.

Sky kisses his wife passionately on the head, calming her down. Gently but firmly holding her to comfort and protect.

KANSAS

Mela glances around the small café, observing the area. People stared at her as if she didn't belong or if she was a troublemaker. She sat at the end of the corner, looking at the menu.

What can I get you? The waiter asked, placing the writing pad in front of her.

Just coffee. Mela said

Anything else? asked the waiter.

Mela didn't say anything else. The newspaper folds in half.

EMPLOYEES WANTED. It said in all caps.

$22.00 for a nails clerk

Mela smirks

"Here is your coffee." Said the waiter.

"That was quick." Mela said

Slam! The cup hit the marble table firmly. Mela takes the cup and places it on the side. Continuing to read her newspaper. A man, 5'9, a little rough around the edges, a left gang scar to the right of his corner eye approaches her.

"What's up, baby?" The man said

His voice sounded familiar, but she couldn't really come near as close to remembering who he was.

Before his hands reached to touch her shoulders.

"Ouch". That hurts your stingy bitch

Mela grinned

He sat across from her, glancing at her figure before asking her age. How old are you?

Mela didn't respond, she continued to read her newspaper, but his aura was intriguing, his smell, his vibe. The bad boy style but he was trouble. Would get in the way of what she was trying to accomplish.

"It looks like you on a mission." He quoted

I know a dude right today, Man, got false passports, ID, I mean I did 12 years in prison for my nigga, and I shot 12 guys while I was in the lead in the crips, man. He continues to share his story. Although the story he was telling was substantial. Very well drilled. Very well impressively rehearsed.

Mela circles her newspaper with her expensive Faber Castell pen.

That's some nice tits you got there. I bet they are milky and soft. Like snowflakes.

Mela was aroused but was closed off to her emotions.

Tell me more about your "homeboy" and where can I find him.

The man leaned in, glancing at her cleavage.

You're not a cop, are you?

Mela smiles

OLATHE, KANSAS CITY

Chapter II

KENA PEACE: 16-YEAR-old the Arson princess

Kena walked into the counseling office without an appointment. The judge said she had to be there for anger management. The reputation she had was arson but without getting caught. So, she came boldly to the office. Interfering with her counseling client. Get up bitch! Kena protested. The girl got up confronting Kena. Kena busted her head against the wall multiple times before the therapist said stop in demand.

An hour later. The therapist placed her pen onto the paper, taking notes. Kena sits on the couch comfortably scraping her nails with the nail picker.

What would you like to talk about today? The therapist asked with an agitated tone. Kena smiles.

"I have other clients that I need to intend to and if you're not going to talk-." Kena puts her hands in the air to stop her from being insulted.

The judge sent me here because of anger. I don't have anger issues. I didn't ask to be here. "Why am I here?" asked Kena. Lighting her up a cigarette.

According to your record that the judge granted me to have. You violently stabbed your boyfriend 5 times but thank God he survived, and with the other three you multiply hit them with the rear end of your car. This causes brain damage, and one can't have children because of his torn testicles and the other boyfriend has stitches all over his face with 50-ounce vodka glass stuck in his throat.

How did you manage hitting the other three with your car again?

I spent 5 years with both at the same time and when I found both cheating at the same time. My main boyfriend came home cheating. I ran out as if I was angry, got in the car. My boyfriend was a slow runner and by the time he came out in the back. "Wham." Kena said

I hit him with the back end of my car. Pretending not to know what forward and backwards meant. Kena laughs at the disaster that she told.

The therapist nodded in understanding.

So, tell me. Does that sound like anger issues? No? asked the therapist.

You can't smoke here. Said the therapist

"And all because you caught them cheating?" Therapist asked

Kena puffs. I hate the law; I hate anyone that provokes someone that has no intention of hurting anyone.

Be specific.

"That is specific you cunt fuck." Said Kena.

What- How did you deal with it?

I stole that cheating bastard car, wallet, checkbooks, spent $5000 during that one week. Sex and alcohol I did for revenge and that shit still didn't make me feel better. Kena said.

I broke his nose. That's how I dealt with it. Now, I'm being charged with assault.

So, your way to handle aggression is through violence? Asked the therapist

Yeah. Kena responded

"What do you want to do with the situation?" The therapist asked in a gentle way but sternly. Straight to the point.

I'm going to kill him." Kena said

"Excuse me?" The therapist raised an eyebrow.

I'm going to have to report that. The therapist wasn't watching at all, Kena stabbed the therapist multiple times before the therapist could defend herself. Blood pulling underneath her. Kena could see her reflection. The door slams.

A night alone. The lighter touches the blunt. Music blasts in the room. her head back exhaling the smoke in the air. Staring at the ceiling, having flashbacks. Kena leans up from her bed, glancing around her room. Silence is what she heard.

A text came through from her boyfriend. In that text was him and the girl kissing. Kena took one more puff. Packing her things. Her parents were never home, her siblings were mean to her. The last thing she needed was a boyfriend that was bold enough to be cold.

Three bubbles started to appear on the screen as a new text was coming through.

The message goes un-responded. A couple of friends left the Berries trailer. The berries brothers were popular. Drunk and loud. In the mist of nowhere. He was a young teen that had his own place. Most likely it was girls and Berries friends who dumps a whole gasoline can on the side of his homeboy's trailer.

Berrie takes a few puffs from his pipe before heading over to his girlfriend. Leaning over for a kiss. Kena starts to throw gasoline onto the windows, on the side. The smell of gasoline she loved and fire she enjoyed. The gasoline that was knocked over wasn't even enough to set them on fire.

Kena left as soon as she could, quickly. While the fire escalated. She glances through her view mirror.

A couple of hours later, the cops came. Along the way out from the city. Firefighters arrive.

Berries' parents arrived once they got the news about their son being in a fire. The father runs to the tragic incident, yelling. While the cops held him back, trying to constrain him.

The forensic pathologists checked to see how many hours was the body buried alive. And it was just for a couple of hours. The father screamed, falling on his knees while he cried his eyes out, suffering with his own tears.

Chapter III

MELA FOLLOWED THE INSTRUCTIONS that the man gave. Into the lowest side of town. Pimps, prostitutes, gangs, broken down building, trashed streets and so forth. Mela came protected.

In a tall ghosted apartment building, the dealer lived in apartment 202. A fenced elevator. Mela pulled the fence to close the elevator, pressing the number 2 button. It elevates but stops in the center but continues to go up.

A blind man with wooden teeth, crooked, smelling like urine and trash stands in the hallway, leaning up against the wall next to the stair case.

"And that's why we take the stairs, you bitch." Said the old man pimp walking. Following her around.

As she walks down the hallway, a dead cat right next to the door of 202.

Mela knocks

The door unlocks right after the first knock.

Are you Charge?

Who asking? Asked a man with a patch over his eye. The man gave the okay for Mela to come in.

I was sent by Fan

"Oh, what can I do for you my love? ." Asked patch.

Passports, ID, Social security.

"Who is you? I never heard of you."

Never mind that. 50Grand. Upfront.

Patch glances through the money, smelling it.

"Smells like peppermint ". Said Patch.

"Well, I like peppermint." Mela said. Finding her wallet in a pile of junk she had in her purse.

Also another 50 Grand to hack my fathers bank system, change my date of birth, and my social security.

" Ma'am, what your asking is impossible. " Patch said . Mela nodded trying to understand but couldn't. She was told that he was the best and that's what she wanted.

" I need that by Friday". Mela said

Maybe you ain't hearing me. I can't hack into your fathers bank, I can't change your social security.

I'm sure you got connections that can help with my social, changing my name, along with date of birth without going to court system.

Everything is done in the court system

And everyone isn't honest in the system either.

I am sure you have felonies that gotten jobs, with a shady clean record that has been erased. And the people that are hiring them doesn't know they were criminals once upon a time. Because you knew someone that knew someone that had higher authority to erase a criminal record from their background check while being in the hiring process, changing their name, social security numbers because their own names, numbers couldn't get any jobs because of their past records.

" What happens to me when I get caught." Asked Patch

"Well, you don't know me." Said Mela

"I knew- I knew this bitch couldn't be trusted ." Patch was stunned. He couldn't believe the stuff that she was telling him. If he gets caught she is no where to be found.

" But all the people you owe to, people that put their work on lines for you. Will be paid in full." Said Mela

" Why- Why do you need all this ?." Asked Patch

"Thank you." Said Mela

Mela sat their waiting for her order to be ready. A couple of hours went pass. Her phone was disconnected. Her parents turned off her phone plan, She couldn't call but they could call her. She takes her battery out of the phone. The designable phone case of a pair of breasts that she painted.

A bomb wire inside the device stuck between the corners of her case. She breathes, looking behind her, glancing the corner of her. Patch bodyguard got suspicious of her. So, he watches her, leaning up against the wall.

Staring at her every move but most importantly, how her curvy hips widened out in the tight dress she had on, along with her straight backbone. When she got up to use the bathroom, she twitched her hips left and right. Her ass fitted well in the dress. Couldn't help but to imagine what was underneath the interest. Had all of patch bodyguards staring, losing concentration. Although, Mela knew what she was doing.

Mela searched for a Bobby pin but nothing was to be found. Three colorful wires that she had to choose to cut from.

It was a small bomb string, how much harm can it be?

Chapter IV

TEXAS

Silk oiled legs criss crossed with Red heels, along two double man pincher on each side of the couch chair. Laying by the woman's feet. Officers taps Mela location with a look alike bombing wire.

Mela was right on their tail once she found out it was a look alike bomb. She cut all three wires. As soon as they lost her. They sighs in frustration.

"We Lost access but the last location was on the east side. Right next to the lowest side of town where officers don't ever go to." Said the officer.

The officer was shyly departed from the others, something different that didn't fit well with Auntie Emerald. Emerald smiled at him, glancing at every part of his body, wishing he would give her warrant but he was young and a rookie. Using him to her advantage would be long gone. Being a cougar and dating a rookie officer wouldn't be for the living.

Auntie Emerald sips her wine as the officer approaches her. He smiles as he passes by. Auntie Emerald gives the look In return. Until the captain of the team disturbs the lustful vibe between the two.

" What could be important ?." She asked

We can't find your niece anywhere.

Keep searching I am sure she is in that same area. Auntie Emerald swallowed whole from her shot glass that was left of the tequila. Slamming it down onto the marble sitting stand.

Fake stumbling her way to the officer. The officer gave a smirk. Trying his best not to give in into her trap of heat but he couldn't resist. How could anyone?

Chapter V

MELA SAT BY HERSELF in a lobby where she waited for a couple of hours for her job interview as a waitress. The clocked turned to 9:30 AM close to her appointment but the time was moving slower and slower while she kept on staring at the clock, hoping and praying that it was 10. Her stomach gave into knots. Other waiters walking by with client's food made her a little bit hungry herself. She couldn't barely think of another hamburger going into another stomach while hers was growling for it.

Mela gets up, staring directly at her phone. Avoiding all contacts while people glanced her way. While Kena walked passed Mela, not paying attention. At the same time they bumped into each other.

" Oh, my apologizes." Kena said

Mela scoffs. Walking away. Kena eyed her closely as she sat where Mela was sitting at. Looking for a piece of paper that was hidden underneath the food menu. Where a tip of money was wrapped up in an envelope and with chip record. Wiping down all the finger prints that Mela left on that table before she vanished to go to another seat

Heavy set lady, 5'8, 246 pound, long black hair, medium thick walked up to the side of the door, disturbingly chewing gum, you couldn't help but to hear it. . People mistakenly took her as for Marilyn Monroe. The only thing that was missing was she wasn't no toothpick. Mela caught herself staring at her luxurious, juicy, big thighs and hips. Her strong shoulders and her big gigantic breasts that stood out mostly with her open V t-shirt.

Mela swallowed her lustful cravings and focused on why she was there. The lady called Mela up, popping her gum.

Mela nods

The lady waited for Mela to walk up first and then she was going to walk behind her. At every opportunity the lady was staring Mela down as if she didn't belong or as if she was interested in Mela too.

The lady whisper" Bubble butt" she whispered before Mela went in. The manager waited for Mela to take her seat. Patiently, he folded his arms, giving her an impatient smile.

" Now, looking at your application. Miss, Temla Peel." He stumbled onto the word, carefully reading before he spoke her name.

" It's very impressive." 4 years in Nursery and 2 years as a banker." He nodded in approval. Closes the file, papers flew across the way towards her. Mela stooped to pick up the paper. The manager looked to see if he could see underneath her blouse as it was a low cut shirt.

Manager sweats trying to keep his composure but it was hard. He was the only guy working there. Working with a bunch a females. It would get any guy hard. Hard to function his daily duties as a manager. Of course he was an older man that wanted a piece of a cherry pie but being married to an old apple pie wasn't as tasty as a Mango Pie. The ladies was like different flavors to him. He would order just pies. No other sweets.

Every lady had a fruit but some were deadly. He just need to find the right deadly one to find out all ladies are not sweet but at his age. He probably already knew.

" Can you cook?." Asked the Manager

Mela nodded. Yes, I can cook.

The manager sighed. Can you clean?

Mela stuttered before she could speak.

Umm, yes. She answered slowly but surely.

mmm-hmm. Before I can hire you. I'm going to need to do a background check. To see if there isn't any criminal records or anything like that. The boss of this restaurant is quite specular of who he hires."

"He likes to inquire his workers." The manager says.

I promise you will be hearing from me pretty soon." The manager added before he placed his reading glasses on his face, getting back to his paperwork. Mela took the hint that it was time to go.

"Uh- Thank you."

The lady waited for Mela outside the door. Giving her a yea right look expression before she even look her way/

Your real name isn't Temla Peel is it? Asked the lady

"What business is it to you?." asked Mela.

" Take a walk with me."

Around the back they headed. The sign on the door says " Smoking deck."

Couldn't miss it.

Who are you really?

Who are you? Mela ignored the question, puffing the vapor she had in her hand.

" Look Miss Temla peel." The lady said. Not believing any words that she was giving.

" I have lived on this earth for 57 years, I know when someone is living a double life sugar. " Said the lady

Mela shook her head in disbelief . Feeling disrespected and called out. Although she kept it together listening to her elders wisdom.

The lady finally stopped talking.

" Are you done?." asked Mela

"Bitch, do you see me talking." The lady replied back.

" Now, I am here to get a job." Mela paused gathering her words together

Who doesn't need one to survive ? Mela continued

"True." The lady half agreed to her statement, observing her with one last snare look.

Mela passed by the lady blowing the smoke in her face while she went inside.

Kena was across the room waiting for the manger to come see her. That same lady that interviewed Mela in a rude awakening way was directing her to the manger way in the back. Towards the back kitchen where the workers was obviously making a mess, causing too much noise.

" As you can see Kena, we really need the help. " The lady said.

" I am Mayi, the look-alike Marilyn Monroe ." Mayi said

I can tell you are genuinely living for your truth. Mayi continued

" How would you know that?." Kena asked

" There is no change name on your resume and your resume hasn't been tampered with by the government . " Mayi said smiling at her with lust, glancing at her up and down.

Mela tsks hearing the conversation . All along that Marilyn Monroe look alike had a name and knew it was changed from the original name. That's why she was questioning her.

That's why she got along with Kena. Knowing she is wanted for arson, 3 degree murder. She comes here where officers come to get a cup of coffee , Old women grannies gossip of who is on the wanted list, who was in the church the following Sunday . Of all places why would she be here?

Kena took the hint of what Mayi was giving her and stared at her reflection in the mirror where the tv was behind her. On the flat screen was a medium size picture right next to the news reporter. While she explained the fugitive details of Kena being wanted.

The server behind the counter turned up the value.

News reporter quotes " If you see this person please call 911.

Majority people that was paying attention knew she was there but still didn't say anything.

" Right this way, sugar. " Mayi assisted

Shoving Kena to the back before the cops came or any fans yelling.

This feels like a movie that I am in. Kena thought

Mayi switched files before the manager came in, Kena gives what are you doing look. Mayi nodded as if she was saying " Trust me, Look."

" Give my new customer some water." The manager said sitting in his seat , scooting forward. Looking for his applications .

Mayi- The manager yells, glancing through his things to find the paper work that was shattered over his desk. In the back of him there was more papers on a desk right next to the television . Kena kept calm as the news came on, going onto the next segment. Kena Peace they showed. The manager was close enough to see Kena's picture.

Kena sips her water while the manager continues to reach for papers from his seat. Drastically falling from his chair onto the paper that was flooding down from the desk to the floor. Kena tilts from her seat smoothly, checking to see if he was okay but continuing to sip her water in a coffee cup.

" Oh, My God sir you okay?. " Yelled Mayi

Startling Kena. Kena caught her water before it spilled over her new outfit from Fashion Nova.

Kena continues to sip her water, glancing at Mayi trying her best not to chuckle. Accidentally turning off the tv he leaned over. Finding his balance but he couldn't . Before he could see, Mayi was helping him up.

" Oh Lord, sorry about that. " The manager said

Mayi gave him the application that didn't have Kena's name on it. So she wouldn't get arrested.

Kena continued to sip her water.

Officers was close to the hallway but was called by another waiter. The waiter had a crush on one of the officers. Mayi grabbed Kena out of her seat, struggling to run out the door, in the back of the kitchen they ran into, Kena, finally got loose to grab herself a bucket of well-done chicken.

" Come on." Mayi yelled for Kena.

Gripping Kena hands real tight. When she saw the officer of the back of the diner. She pushed Kena into the women's single bathroom.

The officer approaches her, hesitating to move passed her. Mayi was acting so suspect. The officer gave a concerning look.

" You okay?" The officer asked

Kena hits the officer to the ground with the wooden door. The officer falls down with one hit. Light headed he was. Mayi and Kena drags him into the women's bathroom.Tearing off his clothes.

Kena grabbed his keys. In the mirror she nods to herself before she headed out.

" You must go now." Mayi demanded

Kena spread red velvet lipstick on her lips

Mela glanced at her watch. From where she was sitting she glanced at the hallway where the manager office was.

The interview was only 5 mins depending if he liked you or not. What was taking Kena so long and why was Mela was waiting up for her? What did Mela want or what did she have in common with her?

Kena walked out the bathroom as a police officer. Mayi gave a smile running behind her. While Kena was close enough to escape. Other officers scoped the police car out.

Kena gave a nod to the other officers before driving by. The other officers drove to the diner. The other officer's partner ran out once seeing his partner down. Calling in backup.

While in excitement of the officer. Trying to shoot the police officer car that Kena was in. He shot Mayi. Before Kena drove towards a highway loop.

The car screeches its tires. Kena watches as Mayi slowly staring right at Kena as she hits the marble ground. Kena placed her sunglasses on after getting a good look at the officer and the officer getting a good look at her.

Chapter VI

THE OFFICER SAT IN the captains officer, nervously shaking his knees. The captain walked in giving one of his best officers some water.

The captain sighs, folding his hands onto his desk. Now, are you sure that it was Kena Peace you saw?

The officer gripped his paper cup into a ball where the water spilled out.

"Captain, Have I ever... Ever lied to you? "The officer paused while saying his sentence. Staring at his wedding ring.

No, you have not? The captain said but gave a confusing look.

"But why would you shoot at a well-known fugitive?." Asked the captain. Leaning against his chair, sipping his coffee.

Officer Locker Street, I know your reputation but there was other ways to handle this situation." The captain continued.

"why not alert the officers, give the car description, and States plate? Go chase the car?" The captain stated.

Officer Locker looked down at his wedding ring, sighing in distress.

"Are you going to arrest me?. "Asked Locker

"We are trying to prevent that now". The captain quickly dialing the phone.

Close the door on your way out? The officer added.

Officer Locker

"Oh, Leave your badge until further notice." Said the captain

Locker jerkily took off his badge, accidentally cutting himself where blood showed. He stared at the blood before wiping it off. Opening the door with his sore hand, leaving the door bloodily.

Officers in the unit stared at him while he walked past. Locker ignoring all disgusting looks while he headed to the locker room.

The locker room was silent. Other officers quickly walked out while he walked in. In the back of him. A 6-foot built man creeped behind him.

"You going to ass fuck me or something." Locker teased.

The ground Locker landed on with one hit by the built man. The man was taller than the others, more built and around the unit he was named the built man.

"You lucky it wasn't one of my daughters." The other officer said walking out the locker room.

Locker groaning, coughing trying to get up.

Locker's brother walked in, placing his gym bag down to help him up. Locker shoved his young brother to the side.

"Don't need your help, virgin. " Said Locker bumping into his baby brother.

Their mother waiting outside against a red charger.

"Get in the car." Locker's mother said.

The car pulled off from the police station, speeding off.

"Would you like to explain to me how you got indicted from the police station?." His mother asked.

"Indicted?" Locker Questioned

"Yes, Jerk. Induced, you were accused of a serious crime you didn't do. "His mother continued.

"That Kena Peace Bitch." Locker Mumbled

"Excuse me, speak up." Sweet Said

"Mama, I don't know- Sweet interpreted his thoughts.

"What does Kena Peace have anything to do with you shooting a 52-year-old woman, Locker. Sweet Voice grew a pitch higher.

" It's complicated. "Locker said

"Boy, you better uncomplicate this shit because you will be going to prison or worse for some complicated shit that you claim is complicated. "

Locker looked at his mother confused.

As they go onto a design highway. Kena was on the other highway that collaborated with where Locker was.

Kena speeded up to their car. On the passenger's side Kena stared Locker down until Locker looked up.

Finally after a while Locker looked up. The same look she gave when she drove off. After he shot the waiter.

" Speed the car up that's her. Locker Exclaimed.

Before his mother could see, Kena was gone turning into another loop highway.

Sweet pulled the car over.

"Who the fuck was that?. She asked.

"I don't know what is going on with you but you need to get yourself together. In the meantime sit back and enjoy the ride. " Sweet demands before Driving off.

Kena pulled up to another state, to a gas station to get some gas. Kum and go the sign said.

Kena pulled something off to disguise her. She stops and thinks before anything. She fixes herself up, pushes up her girls together before getting out the car without no disguises.

Going into the gas station, going into the gum aisle. Grabbing a couple of gum before she heads out.

Throwing a $20.00 down onto the counter where he could grab. 75 cents each right? Kena asked.

The man had an attitude with her before she walked in, glancing towards the TV. Then back at her. Kena gave a smile, popping her gum.

The clerk cleared his throat before he said anything. Seeing that gun on the counter made him think differently before making a scene.

" Thank you for shopping here. He says

Kena nods with a smile

Pumping her gas. The man stares at her from the window on the phone.

Kena calmly gets in the car. Before she pulls off. He realizes that the money that she gave him was a fake. The officers arrived 20 mins later.

Mela sat up after a couple of hours from the back seat. She waited until they were clear away from the scene.

" You are one bold mean bitch. " Mela said. Rubbing her eyes

Kena jerks the car over, swerving.

"What the fuck are you doing- who are you?. " Kena asked

Never mind that. Mela said climbing into the front seat.

" How long were you back there? Asked Kena

Long enough to know that officer killed that Waiter. Trying to shoot at you while you were getting away.

Locker Street was the officer. The officer that shot at you, that shot Mayi Honey.

"Mayi Honey?. " That's that girls name. Kena asked in disbelief.

"Who are you Oh I can't believe it. Sky Juneau Daughter?." Kena questioned.

The commissioner Sky Juneau?

Mela sighed

" Yes, my father is Sky. My name is Mela Juneau.

" You bad girl. Your on the missing child list. Amber Alert has my phone buzzing with notification.

" Are you going to turn me in?. " Asked Mela

Kena side glanced at her then back on the road.

" No, why should I?." Asked Kena

"Well, good, because I can be a help to you a lot.

Kena Scoffed

"How so?."

"You want revenge to whoever killed the kind waitress. Although she was no help to me.

"And?" Kena asked wanting to know more information.

" Locker Street father owes 5 banks through the state of Kanas. We could Rob his estates and Insurance. Now, we may have a little trouble doing so. 5 stages up where he hides all his cash, licenses, etc in one vault. All the original copies are at his bank.

Kena smiled.

" What do you have against Locker Street? " Asked Kena

" He killed my brother 6 years ago. " Mela says

And now he is a cop that killed a waiter at the small café diner for cheering you on for escaping.

Kena pressed on the gas.

" He going to blame it all on you because you were there. He going to make it sound as if she stood in front of the bullet to save your life or something.

" I barely knew that girl. " Kena exclaimed

" That doesn't matter. " Mela said as she glanced over to Kena

Kena observed the road, paying attention to her surroundings

" May I ask you a question? Why did you decide to run away, have one of my people change your name? ."

" A friend of mine pinned a murder on me. We went to a party, she drugged him. Gave me the cup, and said it was for her boyfriend. They found my fingerprint on it. " Mela said

Kena Chuckles

" Charged me with premeditated murder." Mela says

" So, I use my dad's resources, and connections to help me clear my name by changing my name from the system so I can go to college, and have a better life.

Kena nodded in approval

" Premeditated murder, huh?" Kena Questioned

And you say her fingerprints weren't on the cup that she gave you to give to her boyfriend?

Mela nodded

" Are you sure that her fingerprints wasn't removed by acid or something? Even if the fingerprint is wiped down by a clean cloth. The person that touched the cloth has its fingerprints on it. Could leave them to place their prints on the glass. That could lead them to manslaughter. Kena explained turning the corner.

Kena continued to explain

" Unless they were wearing gloves, DNA Gloves. "

" WHAT ?" Mela yelled

" Have you seen the movie Colombiana ?." Asked Kena

"No, I don't think I have. Mela said

" In the movie, the character wore some DNA Gloves that looked exactly like her actual skin. And when she was cleared she took them off and left them between two police cars. " Kena continued

" The reason why I am saying this is because your so-called homegirl must have made some custom DNA Gloves that matched her skin reflection. Whatever dirty job you do, you always wear those gloves and that's what happened. They couldn't trace her prints because she had hers protected. Can't buy those gloves anywhere.

Mela leaned back against her seat, letting the information that was given seek in. Smacking her teeth in anger.

They pulled up to a small house, where an elderly lady was rocking in a wooden chair. Smoking her cigarette.

" Why are we here?" asked Mela

" I am here to pay my respects, get out of the car. You will be my witness if anything goes down.

Kena and Mela walked to the porch together.

" I have been expecting you. " The elderly lady said

Opening the door for both of them. The elderly lady's house had nothing but dishes, music, and family photos of her family. Especially her daughter Mayi.

Mela did her condolences by doing her Catholic prayer.

Kena waited for the Lady to say okay for her sit.

The Lady assisted her to the couch to sit on. Without Kena asking pouring Kena a cup of tea.

" You will love it, it's from Britain " The flavor is exquisite. " Please try some. The Lady said

Kena nodded while she sipped

" I am sorry for your loss, Mrs. Honey," Kena says taking a deep breath

"My daughter has been a fan of you since you became this famous wanted fugitive. This Natural born killer thriller movie vibe of yours. " Mrs. Honey continued

The only thing you didn't have was a partner. Mrs. Honey stared at Kena before glancing back down to her tea. Repressing her tears.

" I was there when that officer killed my daughter. Miss Mae and I were sitting with our church hats on gossiping about the pastor sleeping with one of the group singers at church. I had this feeling that something was wrong. A Mothers intuition. Mrs. Honey said

That's when I looked out and there you were taking an officer's car with sneaky over her. Mrs. Honey glanced over to Mela

Mela looked down at her blouse. Avoiding the awkwardness in the room. Kena gave a smile but quickly gave a no-fun expression of a look back to Mrs. Honey.

" I am a few of the commissioners in this state that know the other commissioner's entitlements.

Mela took Kena's cup to sip on while she knew she was about to hear some juicy stuff. Holding the cup to her mouth while staring at Mrs. Honey before drinking the tea she took from Kena.

" I have a job for you. " Mrs. Honey says

Kena leaned forward.

" I want you to heist the street family, frame Locker Street where he loses all connections, and kill most of his colleagues with his gun by using DNA Protection.

How- How – how do you expect us to do that? Asked Mela

"Well, Miss Juneau your family is well connected I'm sure you can think of something. "

" After the job is done, you can have the money, split a quarter of a trillion dollars between the both of you. I will handle the rest. There will be some conflict along the way and I am sure you can handle it.

Kena didn't ask any questions. She swallowed the rest of the tea in the cup.

" Aren't you going to ask me how you going to get in?.

As we speak Sweet Street arrives at her husband's bank around 10:55. She gets off at Highway 55 goes down the street speeds into the corner by 11:01. Wears the same heels every day. Different suit though.

Mela sips her tea, slurping playfully.

Mrs. Honey waited for her to finish

Kena stared at Mrs. Honey forcing a smile. Once Mela was done Kena yanked the cup from Mela as Mela was resisting to let go.

" Trillion dollars will be on each floor if you can get access with a fingerprint of some kind. You can get access. I want this done in two days. Empty out their estate, kill Locker's colleagues of his connections, and bring me, Locker, himself.

Mrs. Honey sipped her tea. Kena and Mela begin to walk out together until they heard steps behind them. They stop. If any intruders butt in our plan. I will make sure to assassinate them. Family or not. And Miss, Juneau you will find out why you were betrayed. Mrs Honey says as she was behind them. Kena and Mela had their back turned while she spoke. When she was done they both walked out in Union.

As they enter the car, speeding off.

Mela took a deep breath.

" DAT BITCH KNOWS WHO FRAMED ME!." Says Mela

Kena kinda had a clue who. Where the person that tried to frame her, tried to do it to Kena once upon a time but Kena wasn't an easy target.

"Ooooh, just wait until I see that bitch. " Mela says

Kena says nothing throughout that day.

Chapter VII

LOCKER STARED AT THE ceiling in his room as the fan continued to circulate through the room. He throws the basketball into the air and catches it. His father knocks on the door before entering.

His father sighs as he exhales before speaking. Gathering his thoughts.

"You're a 30-year-old man has his own home, car, wife. And for him to be in this situation hurts my pockets deeply. "His father says sitting on lockers bed

The locker sighs in disgust.

"As a commissioner of this state and as your father I will do everything in my power to get you out of this drama, but you must do something for me in return. "Kill that, Kena Peace. She is bringing stress to my community. "His father continues before existing the door

Coming back with more demands he peaks through the door.

"In meantime and between time, pull yourself together and avoid trouble. "His father says

The locker waits until he leaves before flipping him off.

Jail bars lock. Locker waited for his homeboy in the visiting room Behind a glass he wasn't used to. It used to be where they would be across the table from each other, the inmate in handcuffs, but this was their reality.

His homeboy picked up the phone, placed it to his ear.

"What's up, Street? "His Homeboy Tough said

I heard that you were on trial for the murder of Mayi Honey! That's impressive dawg. Tough say

"I don't see how. "Locker says

"Well, you will place as police brutality, although the victim was not black. You still killed an innocent standby. According to the news hear say".

Tough tapped his fingers on the concrete. Tusking shaking his head playfully

You are well connected. I'm sure with a little time in jail and some probation you will be fine. Although that hard work at the police academy will be suspended and you will no longer be able to apply as an officer of any state you may choose to go to in the future. Your record will forever be discovered. And you being on the news will always be worse.

"If that Kena Peace Bitch wasn't there. "Man, that bitch is a distraction. "Locker said

"Get me some hot wings and a hamburger. Tough demanded

Officers escorted them into a private room, bringing some food. Locker grabbed him a plate.

"Uh huh homeboy, all this is mines." Tough added grabbing himself a plate

"This Kena Peace Chick, leave her alone man. She is a famous fugitive that is wanted for arson and Murder. "Tough said

"So?" Locker shrugged

"What personal odds do you have against this woman?" Asked Tough

"She killed my partner at the coffee diner. "Said Locker.

"No, she knocked him out. "Tough corrected

It was until after you killed Mayi his heart stopped, which was weird. He had brain damage due to past abuses from his childhood and once she knocked him out, he was still breathing. She was just trying to get away. And in her case. I don't blame her. "Tough said taking a bite of his chicken

"Anyone in my way would've been hurt too. Trying to keep me away from escaping. You will get hurt." Tough explained

"What your point? ." asked Locker

"Your problem is that you want that $50,000 reward that they got on her. Knowing damn well you ain't going to get that reward as an officer. You might have gotten a raise for catching her but not the $50,000 reward they promised. Come on man, y'all a bunch a show and tell anyways. "

Locker took a deep breath to what he was saying.

"You just wanted the money, and I don't know how you thought by shooting her was going to get you that 50 grand.

Locker quickly pushed her chair back, grabbing the food.

"Hold up, hold up, leave the bucket of chicken and Potato salad, dawg." Tough said as they both were tugging war for the food. Finally, Locker gave up, leaving the food with tough.

"He got me fucked up, this potato salad good. "Tough complimented as he chewed his food.

Locker was almost on his way out the gate but stopped midway. He was right. Locker didn't have any personal conflict with Kena. She is wanted for murder and there is 50 grand if found alive.

Locker walked back to the private room.

"You done being butt hurt now?" Asked Tough

Locker cracked a smile as he looked towards the prison bars

"Can I have a plate now?." Asked Locker

If you have washed your hands? Tough chuckled

During his visit his mother continued to call during his visit. Locker placed his phone in silence.

Locker and Tough enjoyed their visit.

Kena and Mela were outside his family's bank. Scooping the place out. Mela wore her sunglasses so she would not be recognized. While Kena didn't care about it. People were after her, people wanted her. She was famous, she was talked about, hated on, loved on. She grew tough skin and some balls.

Let's go! Kena said

Well, hold up. Mela held her arm to stop her. Using her eye vision glasses.

Two security guards up front. And a couple inside with heavy duty armor. The armor truck is over there probably got security cameras that match people's faces that work there. Highly technical security, Miss Peace. Mela checked Kena quickly. Kena placed her one foot back into the car, slamming the door, glancing at Mela up and down.

We gotta think this through, why on earth would she pick us? Mela gave a questionable look.

"I am straight up killer that doesn't mind killing. I am a contractor that gets paid for killing other commissioners and precisely I get reckless. I don't clean up after my mess and that's why I am wanted for murder. Kena explained that clearly

And I am- Mela Paused

"A girl that is illegal trying to change her name, her background without having the government getting involved or knowing about it because she was falsely accused by her so-called home girl of drugging her homegirl's boyfriend. " Kena answered her.

"Right!" Mela slowly agreed

Not believing that Kena was a contractor.

"You're not planning on killing my father, are you? Asked Mela.

Kena tried her best not to hurt the poor lost girl, but she didn't want to lead Mela to a stray.

"If the qualifications call for it. " Says Kena.

Mela took a deep breath, her heart trembling.

Let's get real, your father is the only reason that you're in this mess.

Mela wasn't paying attention to detail like Kena ways. Mela father Sky Juneau walking out of the Streets estate with Sweet Street, getting in the same car as her.

While they share a decent friendly kiss while the car drives off. Kena smacked her lips while she drove away.

A call popped up on Mela's phone

Mrs.Honey the caller ID said

Answer it

Mela answered

"Turn that car around and do the job. I have my men on each floor that will deliver the money to you.

Kena turned the car around. Speeding up. A police car followed them as she broke down the speed.

"Don't worry about them, just get to the bank before they close it by 2. That is when the delivery will be dropped off by the armor truck.

Another car crashed into the police car. Two massive shooters got out of their vehicles and shot at the officer's car. While innocent by standers ran for their life. The two shooters couldn't be identified as they wore black Amor Masks.

Mela sneaked in the back as she knocked out one of the armor workers. Getting in headfirst and not the tail. The security guard stopped Mela as if she was an intruder.

Her head continues to stay down to disguise herself.

The security let her pass as she went to her job section. Collecting each associate's estates as she glanced through each of Lockers Investors. She kept reading. She ran into her father's name. In shock she was. Right under the name of of her father. The girl that framed her. Maeve Play

She quickly gathered the documents and placed them into a Ben and left that locker. Each of the 3 lockers she cleaned out. While Kena was cleaning out the rest, following Mrs. Honey's instructions. Kena quickly gathered her things before heading out. Ditch the car you drove, take the company's car.

Locker hanged with his homeboy until his time was up. The fried crispy chicken was gone.

"Watch who you hang around, watch your livelihood. There are people out to get you. "Tough warned

But Locker laughed it up as if it was a joke. Tough didn't smile while he left. He just nodded.

Chapter VIII

FLINTON KEEN WAS A 65-year-old man that lived in a nice mansion amongst the hills of Kansas. Gated community he ensured. Too righteous to live amongst the regular rich folks. He had young girls every week that he screwed while his wife was running campaign to be the next commissioner president of a children's club. Of course, nobody really brought into that mess except for the rich scheme folks. It was more likely for Flinton to have 5 girls at a time during his sex sessions but this time he had two.

As a window cleaner Kena pretended to be. The man was well connected. Could bankrupt good lawyers, have drug dealers become doctors all by just one phone call and it was done. Kena hesitated for a second. Thinking that this man could be a use to Mela, but business was business. She was given a order to kill him first.

The list of investors was Locker's connections. If they are dead, he has no other connections that he grew up with that he would personally know. Other connections, investors from out of state were enemies of his fathers. And couldn't possibly help him if he was in need. So, Locker stuck to what he knew.

Kena climbed the stairs that lead to the front door. Knocked on door. One of his chicks opened the door.

"Yeah?." The young girl said nonchalantly

I'm here for 3 o'clock clean up.

Oh yes, my apologies he is expecting you.

Kena walked observing the place, thinking when the last time she saw luxury or had it. Although she got paid good money herself. She was a con artist along with being a contractor.

"Haven't you seen a mansion with good things before? "The girl asked

I better get started. Kena replied

On what? The girl asked.

The girls were beautiful looking but dumb and stupid. She was obviously there to clean the windows.

In the nick of time Lana Del Rey Born to Die album starts to play and One of his girls was dead. One more to go.

As the music played loud over the speaker. They couldn't hear anything. Along with the loud moaning the girl was giving. While the couple was having intercourse, Kena shot both. Double killed them with one silent shot. Kena stared at them, smiling.

Fast walking through the hallways that she remembered but she didn't have any time to reminisce. Mela waited for Kena as she was the driver.

Without a word Mela drove off.

Crossing out each investor that was dead with the fingerprint of Lockers.

27 more investors to go and we have until Tuesday.

Kena was the only one recognizing the thing that Mela would miss.

A Strip club fan was parked in the bushes. Clearly a van with two naked girls as an advertiser picture for their business.

Kena chuckles, laughing. Not remembering the last time, she laughed. Mela laughed at her laugh as her laugh was laughable to laugh at, but Kena kept that serious interior as she glanced at the van that was glancing at them.

After work, how about a little play at the strip club? Asked Kena

Mela gave her Are you joking look. Held that look for a few seconds until Kena looked her way.

What?

"And how do you expect us to get in without ID's?" Mela said

I have my resources. Kena replied

Chapter IX

THE STRIP CLUB WASN'T full, and They wasn't taken no prisoners. Showing no mercy. The security guards waiting for client's ID's. It was a free club. You paid for drinks and services instead. Which made it fun. Mela and Kena walked together as if they were a lesbian couple.

Before the security guard even asked for Identification. Without a word, both guards were on the ground. Kena repeatedly hitting him. Mela talking as she was hitting him with her empty purse.

Mela stopped herself. " You should be ashamed of yourself. " Mela randomly said, losing her balance, fixing her hair.

Mela had to stop Kena from not killing the guy.

"Calm yourself. "

"Hell Nah." Kena replied back

Remember why we're here.

"I also said for a little play at the strip club."

A half-naked stripper slid down the pole, with her tongue licking the pole as she slid down, climbing back up again. Swirling with her legs into a V shape.

Kena smiled, taking a drink that wasn't hers and drinking it. That the waiter was going to give to someone else. Which was another client. The hair of the stripper was guarding her face.

As soon as you know it, Mela was at the table, mistakenly taken as the birthday girl. Carried by the dancing men. Placing her on the back. Trying to get loose, tequila was poured on the stomach. Although she wanted to say no. The sexual treatment she never had.

Kena shook her head smiling. Keeping her eyes on that one stripper that guarded her face a lot.

Excuse me, how much for a private room? With that stripper.

"150.00. "The waiter says.

Kena nods

"Very Good."

Two men walk the stripper back to the back.

It's her. It's Mela Juneau. The stripper said in unbelief

How did she find me? Let me call Locker. See what he says

The phone was busy and all she got was the dial tone.

AUSTIN'S FOOTBALL PARTY

Cocaine was passed around in the circle. The Truth and Dare turned into a drug abuse high heaven and hell win win. As one of his friends lined the coke up in a line, everyone cheered for Locker to snort it. Watching, taking photos. Locker was gathered with three girls without even knowing it. Drinking Ciroc drink along with three shots of Hennessy. Spiked with Molly and Heroin.

Some passed the heroin around in a blunt but passed it right back to Locker as he was already passed out. Now it was the right time to ask the stupid questions.

So, Locker. How was killing Mayi? Did you fuck her before you killed her? Was the pussy tight?

Locker smiles while answering.

She sure was Shorty. With one bang.

One of Austin's friends was getting frustrated. Pulling his homeboy aside.

"HE IS ISN'T-CONFESSING ANYTHING YET."

Give it time

The phone continues to ring. The stripper continues to call him but no answer.

THE STRIP CLUB

A lady of impeccable importance wore a white dress in VIP. Kena couldn't help the posture she carried. Another waiter interrupted Kena's thoughts.

That's Marble Tune. One of the highest ranks in Kansas. Married one of the Commissioners.

Which Commissioner? Asked Kena

The waiter shrugged, walking away. "Have a nice night. "She added.

Two ladies kissed in front of marble. Kena approached Marble, grabbing a drink off the table that belonged to her.

"That seems cheap." Kena says

The two ladies got up without Marble saying anything. Impressed.

Kena continued to stand in her power.

Once Kena introduced herself. She was interrupted.

"I know who you are, Miss Peace. What can I do for you? "

The stripper peaked out from the sink curtains, panicking.

I got to get out of here.

Locker was still knocked out. Not knowing where he was. He was hyper awake but hyper asleep. He would wake up knowing what he was doing but doze off every time.

The others laughed at him as he pisses on himself.

"Come on Girls, take a ride in my Maserati. "Locker says waking up sanely but dozing off slagging to the floor.

The boys followed him. Locker was high, he couldn't remember anything.

THE STRIP CLUB

The club was in the middle of closing. Mela took a nap in the middle of the performance. Everyone passed by her as she slept. The owner had to wake her up.

The stripper ran into the back of the alley. Her heels trembling over.

Why was she running? What was she afraid of?

Was Mela more dangerous than she led on? Where was Kena? Mela? Who was working for who?

An intruder stops her. It was hard to see the kidnapper's face. As they grab her to place her in the Van.

Waking up from a hit on the head. It was blurry. She only saw two men standing in front of her.

At the same time, she woke up. Locker did too.

2 WEEKS LATER

The girl from the strip club woke up. Whatever they gave her was strong enough to knock her out for a couple of days or weeks. They seduced the pain pills so it wouldn't kill. Not knowing what her punishment would be.

Flashlights on the car turn off once the Lincoln Navigator pulls up. Red heels stepped out of the car. The heels clapped on the concrete floor. A red luxury suit shined through as soon as she stood underneath an old dusty lamp.

As the lady wore sunglasses. Red lipstick, chewing bubblegum that smelled like cherries and hair too wet as if it was soaked down with gel.

She posed with her legs apart, staring at the girl hanging. Popping her gum again. Walking away to her car. Buttoning up her suit.

The girl only saw blurs. Mela walked up to the girl, smiling.

I never did think this day would come. 5 years I did in juvenile until I turned 16. My parents had the money to put me through school while I was locked up. Teachers came by to see me but not one of my friends did. I only had two. You and Keyila. Then keyila died of a hit and run.

Mela scoffed in unbelief

A friend of mine gave me a drink to give to her boyfriend, drugged him and blamed her best friend for killing him, played the victim of lost lover.

Mela cocked her head.

The girl struggled to speak, dozing off to sleep.

Wake her up! Mela demanded

Its Premeditated Murder you stupid bitch. The girl said.

You had it all, all the money, the friends, teachers liked you. And when I found out you slept with my boyfriend behind my back after I asked you to tell me. You lied to my face.

Remember Kiay? The girl that always wanted to be me. Dressed as me, talked like me. Like damn, we looked just alike. Couldn't tell the difference. " Mela said

You mistaken her from me. And you- You wanted to frame me because he like me more. And-

" He was always mines, he- Mela interrupted

Nah, nah, see you and Mate was already over. That's what he said. And Mate never came off as a liar. He was the one that always told the truth. Mela yelled out

I would never ever sleep with my best friends man at all.

Mela sighs. Sitting in front of her. Maeve dangling side to side.

Maeve Play was your name. You changed it once the FBI was after you. Without going to the courts. You illegally changed your name. I did my research.

Maeve stayed silent as she was choking on the rope.

A girl named Urella Keirl she went to juvenile with me for 2 months. Then when you went in. She went in with you. You might know her.

Swinging in circles. Choking to death

Your father asked me to kill you once, but I didn't. I thought framing you was better. She says saying her last words

The look on her face was disgusting. Mela felt released but anger arrived. She had to find out why her own flesh and blood was after her.

Mela flipped a torch and threw it. Watching the flames light up. Smiling as her heart was content. Walking out quickly.

An Uber pulled up just in time before anyone knew anything. Once pulled off. The bomb blew up.

Downtown Kanas had a crowd, protesting, people marching to the speech that a commissioner in that state was making.

People chanted "No Commissioners, No Rights!"

Uber dropped her off at a nice hotel called The Fontaine

Thank you don't forget to rate, Mrs. peace. He quickly said. Mela giving a what in a world look on her face.

Waiting for her to get out of the car. Driving off he did once she slamed the door. Mela staring at the high building that the hotel was made of. Putting her sunglasses on. Her heels stepping in. Placing some pep in her step.

Hello Miss Ji, your room is 145. Do you have any bags that need to be taken up?

Not knowing what was going on. Mela played along. Not answering his question but shaking her head for a response.

145 her room said

The door was already unlocked. Who was there? Closet doors open with clothes. Mela stared at the closet before drawing out her gun. Hesitating. Once she turned to the other side. Kena was fully dressed in her all-black suit.

"This is where we will be camping for now. Your cut will be on the side where your clothes are.

Where are you going? Mela Questioned

"I will be doing some personal business.". Kena says, placing on her watch.

Mela nodded.

Kena walks up, giving Mela her gun.

"If you need this, don't hesitate to use it. " Kena said.

Mela grabs Kena giving her tight squeeze hug.

Although Kena hesitated to give her a hug back. She gave a hug back

"Be Careful." Mela said

Walking out grabbing her cut of money to go with her. Kena walking out without looking back.

Mela fell onto the bed with her arms wide open. Glancing at the ceiling. Taking a deep sigh of release.

Chapter X

THE CLOCK WAS TICKING. People continued to march down the street. Chanting louder and louder. A limo passes by them, they hit the car yelling. One spit on it, others was throwing eggs. While an unbothered protester was standing there silently. Watching the car go by.

Kena jogged down each level of stairs going to the rooftop where the equipment was waiting for her. A phone call comes through. "Make it look like an accident." A women says over the phone.

A dial tone clicked, and Kena waited for Water Street to step onto the stage. People yelled in excitement, raising their flags. While Water was shaking hands with Sky Juneau. Kena raised her head in surprise.

"What was Mela father doing there? Why was he by Street side? 20-year-old rivals support Water Street and for what reason?

Sky hated Water for a very long time. While Sky trained him as his mentor. Water Street gets voted in because of more investors. Investors that he thinks he has.

Holding a precision rifle shooter. Kena zoomed in on the target.

Mela turned on the TV. The news was going live. On the stage Mela saw her father standing right next to Water Street. The father of Locker Street. Mela dropped her coffee mug, looking around in disbelief. Biting her lips in stress.

Kena zoomed extra closer aiming for his head but zooming out. Not wanting to shoot Mela's fathers.

Two shots fired and he was down.

Everyone ran once they heard the gunshot. Secret service calling in on the action. 10 Police cars driving down an empty street. Like a fast and furious movie, they turned the corner.

Just in time for Kena to make her escape. Jogging down the steps again. All elevators were shut down. Kena ended up running with the others, midway stopping at a random car, highjacking the car in broad day light.

It wasn't like anyone was paying attention. Everyone was too busy saving their asses from being shot or worse.

She pulls off, smiling, without any remorse.

Her next stop was a jewelry store.

Taking the money with her, leaving the keys in the random car. Minutes in, the police arrive. Tracking the stolen car. Kena glances behind her but not concerned as she goes into the store. Glancing at some engagement rings.

The assistant nodded at her as Kena glanced around. One ring caught Kena's eye. A big rock diamond square shape for 43K.

"I pick this one." Kena says

LAMBORGHINI DEALERS

Three airplanes flew all at Onces into the pink sunset. Italy Kena was called to come to. Had her name changed but kept the name Kena Peace but for her to go to Italy she would have to change her appearance. Hid the money in another hotel that she was staying at. Only took what she needed most.

Icon was shining looking. Interior design was on point. Speed, power and taste was all Kena was looking for. An Assistant with red nails was touching the car as she walked up to Kena. Smiling at her, glancing at her up and down as if she was lusting for the power Kena had. Attractive.

Kena pointed to the car she wanted. The Lamborghini Huracan.

"Good Choice." The seller said

Signing the paper of where they stood. The seller gives Kena the keys. Kena tightly holding onto the keys. Closing her eyes in relief.

The Garage door opens as Kena drove off.

Back to Kansas City

Into the land was a highway to the customer's house that hired her. Kena parked her car smoothly. Marble steps she stepped on.

THE FONTAINE HOTEL

Mela sniffed her partner's clothes as she was looking through her stuff. Smelling the pear scent that Kena had was impelling, impeccable, strong, witty. She couldn't help but to thrush herself into her clothes. Thinking about Kena holding onto her tightly.

Mela untied her robe. The robe slid off her body. Stepping over the robe. Running the cold water. Half full she steps in. Scooting up forward, she leans back. Going underwater.

Her eyes wide open

Holding her breathe for at least a few mintues. Feeling all the anger she held onto for the last few months, going into flashbacks. Closing her eyes, allowing herself to purge those thoughts. She didn't have a lot of time to reflect on herself while on the run but during that moment she was finally purging her thoughts. Hearing her daddy sing to her when she was little, going back into time where being behind bars was all she knew. She deserved it. An inmate mindset, what she was taught. Being a good friend got her 5 years of premeditated murder. After giving her word to her friend that she recently killed that her loyalty was bond. Being her best friend's ride or die was something she didn't get in return.

She wanted to drown herself right then and there but if she did. The people that wanted her dead would win and there wouldn't be any war to continue.

The more they saw her alive, the more they wanted to bring rousing battles. Each battle that was thrown at her she won. Not knowing what to believe, feeling angry but not knowing what to feel, who to blame her anger for. Herself? For being a good friend? A loyal soldier?

Out of her depression state the door knocked.

Quickly and in a hurry, she got out, grabbing the nearest robe that was hanging from the towel hanger.

The door stopped knocking.

Peeking out the door. Room Service

All clients must leave their rooms for room service.

Mela looked stunned, not arguing.

"Okay just one minute. Mela said as she put on the nearest shirt, pants she saw.

Taking the big tote of money.

MASSACHUSETTS

The Cartier Store

Mela in her focus mood, she was glancing at the jewelry manual. For the engagement ring there was a small ring with 5 diamonds. What Mela had in mind was to buy from online sources. Using her father's account, she had some points to cover. Paid for the jewelry in full. No payment installation.

All she could think about was Kena and her well-being. No calls came by or anything. The ring buzzes. No phone number. Private perhaps? Mela answers.

"Never answer a call you don't know." Kena says

Mela sighs in release.

"Oh, my God, okay you're okay. Mela says

"I am in town but handling business for a customer of mine. Once this is finished, we will go on a trip somewhere. Just me and you. " Kena says

"Yes, that sounds great". Mela says

I love you was going to slip out but instead she kept it inside. Kena blushes as she looks down towards her blouse. Holding the phone to her shoulder. Opening the ring case, the diamond shining as a star.

They both hang up as people approach them.

Mela sips her water while being approached by a customer of hers.

Picture shots were being taken without her knowing it.

"I see you haven't done your job yet. A lady says in a bitter tone.

Mela shrugs, not caring about what the lady had to say, knowing that the lady paid her a good salary for her to turn Kena in. Mrs. Cattie was a mean snake.

"I couldn't do it. " Mela said

"And why not?" asked Mrs. Cattie

"You're in love?" Mrs. Cattie says

Mela slurps her water, giving her a cocky look.

"If you don't do your job, I will make sure that I will do it for you and another thing. Kena was ordered to kill you due to a client's request. Did you know that?" Mrs. Cattie continued.

Without a phase of reaction, she smacked her teeth.

"Are you done, Mrs. Cattie. I would like to continue my drawings and finish my water, if you don't mind." says Mela.

"Gladly." Mrs. Cattie says

Mrs. Cattie walks away, another photo shot was taken once she walked away. Mela flips the camera man off. Another snap.

The sigh Mela held in was let out bitterly. Unfortunately, she was uncomfortable. Heading back to the hotel. The door was locked, and everything was in place. Locking the door behind her.

She stumbles onto this head-solid thing that was nowhere to be found. When she looked underneath the bed. She bends down on her hands and knees to get the phone. The more she tried the more it was harder to reach. Grabbing something more stable was something that she needed.

Hhm she grunts. Finally grabbing it. A phone without a lock screen. Who was it? Was it Kena's? Was it someone else? Did someone leave on purpose? Knowing Kena she would've gotten anything that was important. In today's society, phones are the most important. Who would purposely leave their phone?

Maybe a message that someone was in here? Someone knew she was there, knew who she was, and who she was with.

Mela's finger was almost ready to press but taking her finger back. Not wanting to pry but who wouldn't?

The unlocking sound clicked.

Photos she tapped. Scrolling through was a photo of Urella Keirl her former roommate from juvenile detention. She gasps in surprise. Old photos of who she was and what her mother looked like. Her family looked close. Mela was placing two and two together. Kena was Urella. Umbrella was Kena. Facial surgery records were underneath the name medical records. Whoever had this phone knew who she was and was close to her. Wanting Mela to know this information. Squeezing the phone in anger. Fighting her urges to be angry. She breathed in and out. The lies were making her nauseous, and overbearing. Keeping so many lies was getting unpopular. Everyone had secrets. That's what her father was trying to tell her. Feeling bitter towards her soon-to-be fiancé. Running to the bathroom, vomiting onto the floor as she couldn't make it to the toilet.

Behind her was a man in a mask breathing heavily. Grabbing her by her hair, strangling her. Mela grabs anything that was useful. An unbroken towel hook by her was near. The intruder tried to keep her away from it so she couldn't reach it.

Hitting him in the nuts was the only option. Ripping the hook off the wall. Hitting him repeatedly. Running to her gun, shooting him twice. Once again in the head since the two bullets didn't hit well enough.

Crouching over. By her red toenails, the body lay at the end of her baby toe. Breathing heavily, vomiting on the intruder. Wiping her face A silent call came through.

" Is it done?". An unfamiliar voice came on the phone

Recognizing his voice

" Hello Dad, a visitor came to see me. You tried to kill me, why?." Mela asked

" You didn't want to do anything with your life or the tools that me and your mother were giving you. " Sky said sternly

She hung up

Yelling in anger. Putting the pillow over her face, suffocating her tears, while she tried to breathe.

Leaving the hotel room with her things. Grabbing the stuff her partner had and leaving before getting discovered.

As the real Miss Ji pulled up, the cops were already there. Walking up to the front desk.

"Hello, Miss Ji. Made a reservation for 145.

A Detective approached her

Are you, Miss Ji? Asked the detective

Miss Ji looks confused, putting her hands behind her back.

Come with us." The detective read her rights as they were escorting her out of the hotel.

Excuse us. " The detective says walking out, opening the driver's door to his car.

The Homicide team was detecting the blood.

Trim anything? Asked the Detective

Well, no fingerprints, we have detected two blood stains from a couple of weeks ago. Trim quoted. Continuing to take photos.

"What else?." Asked the detective

Well, repeatedly hitting the intruder, broken door knob, etc. Trim said shaking his head.

"And did you say no fingerprints?." Questioned The detective

The detective crossed his arms, waiting for an explanation.

Trim sighs

" Old people." He stretches but mumbles the words

Trim had two pair of skin-reflection gloves, placing them on as a demonstration. Getting ready to explain the easy-understanding concept.

" In late 2012 they created these DNA gloves where it connects with your DNA to your actual skin. And see?

The gloves fitted along with my skin, you can't tell if it is my gloves. It looks realistic and feels realistic.

On the murder weapon no DNA. Phone? No. Nothing.

And another thing that you professionals forget.

Transferring fingerprints by anything.

No shaking hands.

People don't shake hands because of germs. It's because of someone else fingerprints. Once you shake hands with another human. You're more likely to mix their fingerprints with yours.

Like this vase here, as we run it. A couple of fingerprints have been on here. Even though they have never been to jail. We ran the fingerprints with their footprints. Same DNA and everything. Trim gave a long speech but a understanding one.

" That's why they ask for babies foot prints. " said Trim.

Trim walked away leaving the officer and Detective stunned.

Anyone could have done the murder.

Chapter XI

MRS. SWEET AND MRS. Juneau sat silently in Mae's living room.

"What do I owe this pleasure?." Mrs. Juneau said.

Mrs. Sweet shook her head in disbelief.

"Don't act like you don't know why I am here. " Said Mrs. Sweet

"Why are you here?." Asked Mrs. Juneau.

" Have you heard about the Ireland girls coming to Kanas? Well, if you Haven't. They were kidnapped two months. Signing off deals with Million of Dollar's after being sold to the highest bitter. " Says Mrs. Sweet.

Mrs. Juneau gave a shrug.

"Your husband works very well with mines. Our husbands partners seems a bit close. " Mrs. Sweet says Drastically

Hmm, I am not going to pretend that I want you here. Because I don't." . Mae said with her voice breaking.

Mrs. Sweet showed the pictures to Mae.

Mae refusing to look but slowly glances at the photos.

For months he been fucking with the Ireland girls and since they been kidnapped- Mae interrupted

" And you come to me because? ."

Mrs. Sweet smirks

"Knowing my husband, he aint the type to go down alone without dragging someone with him. Being married to a ruthless Cobra hasn't been easy. " Mrs. Sweet explained

" I'm here to warn you. Protect your assets, protect what you have owed before you got married. Knowing the FBI if they cant get to the husbands. They come for the wives. Using some type of old history against you. From where I know your innocent. " Mrs. Sweet Continued

" Well thank you for the warning but I knew about protecting my assets, my pensions, mansions, my house that I own in Maldives. Owning property from west to North coasts. I knew damn well that my shit had to be protected". Mae raised her glass to her truth.

" For months your husband and mines have been involved in the 5 month trial of the kidnapping. They just haven't discovered who is involved. Found 6 girls dead in one week. Shipping the girls out of state to find their bodies dead underneath some ocean outside of the state.

Mae Laughed tinkled pink as she couldn't be anything she was saying. Not to mention the anger that she felt towards her. Unhealed wounds.

I know we may have had our differences.

Mae raised her eyebrows

But we really need to put that aside and just handle what we need to.

Mae smiled

Speaking dealing with what we need to .

Mrs. Honey walked in the living room confident. Staring at Mrs. Sweet angrily

Mrs. Sweet uncomfortably cleared her throat.

You could feel the tension in the room. The anger, the rage of energy. Nothing else had to be said.

Mae gave kena a smile as she gave her the okay to sit down.

Now, Mrs. Honey is here. And we must put our differences aside, right? Mae says

Mrs. Honey handles our screw-ups, our knowingly fuckups that we do on purpose.

"You may go Kena".

Kena grabbed her money in a suitcase and walked out. Glancing at her clock. Mrs. Sweets car blew up.

Kena walking passed it, getting in hers.

Mela was swimming outside her room. Each client in that hotel had a swimming pool, can' see through glass. Kena watched Mela as she swam in her nice tight bathing suit. Hugging her curves, legs thicker. Mela looked through the glass to see through her room but couldn't see anything. Right, where Kena stood was where Mela stood to look in. At the same time walking away from the glass. The water splashing.

Doing Stokes. Every time Mela did something. She did it with focus, determination. Releasing her stress from whatever she was feeling. The robe slid off Kena, stepping on the pool stairs, meeting her halfway as Mela did her strokes forward.

Mela tilts forward, kissing Kena. Sharing their pent-up passions. Mela jumped onto Kena, wrapping her legs around her in the middle of the pool. Kena walked to the pool window, over the city you could see. Touching Mela with a sense of mystery. Slowly taking off her bathing suit. Leaning towards her neck. Swirling her tongue towards her cleavage.

Mela held her close enough to hug her. Slowly moaning but crying at the same time. Kena sensed something was wrong but couldn't put her finger on it. Sobbing continues and without a word. Kena held her right there in the pool.

Taking their seats, Mela was shaken. Didn't want to be touched by anything. Kena stared at her in concern. Leaning over to her, by the table.

" Did something happen when I was away?. " Kena asked

Mela signed

" My father put a hit on me because I didn't obey him by going to Princeton. What kind of parent would do such thing to their own flesh and blood?." Asked Mela, glancing towards Kena looking for an answer.

No answer could be given to that question. Nobody would have the answer to that but the person that wants them dead.

Did you ask him? Asked Kena

Mela scoffs.

" JUST BECAUSE I DIDN'T OBEY HIM." Mela says shaking her head.

Tears continue to roll down.

" Your Mother says she loves you and she gives you her blessing. " Kena says looking at the sky.

" Don't know how to accept, move forward, or forgive at this point. " Mela says folding her hands together.

" Pray, give it to God." Kena suggested

" Do you know how blessed we are that we made it through the trials of our life and where we are now. " Kena says bending down to Mela. Placing her head onto Mela's lap.

" Did my father send you to kill me? " Asked Mela

Kena swallows their head, closing her eyes. Crying.

" Why haven't you killed me? " Asked Mela

"Because I love you and I want you to marry me. " Kena applied, opening up the ring case

A big-cut diamond shined once the case opened.

" YES! ".In excitement she says. Her mood changed. Feeling the peace that was in that moment.

To the room, they go into.

Mela danced on top of the bed, wiping her hair back and forth. Kena throwing money. They both laugh. The bed was scattered with money. Mela walked over to Kena, grabbing her head to lean against her.

Making Love on the purple fur sheets. Kissing each other passionately. Mela gets on top, pouring oil on her body, the oil slowly sliding on her vanilla skin. Kena smiles, grabbing Mela's, and pushing forward. Moaning they both do.

Mela sighs bouncing up and down. Rubbing her back, holding onto support as she pushes forward. Their eyes lock. Stopping their acts to share an intimate. Mela places her head onto Kena's. Breathing as she continues to swirl.

"I LOVE YOU TOO. " Mela says kissing Kena, towards her neck. Pushing Kena down, leaning toward her chest, licking the honey off her cleavage towards her stomach. A night of passion continued to the next day.

Chapter XII

MRS. SWEET WALKED INTO her husband's office livid. While Water had a meeting with his colleagues. She picked a day to interfere.

"Everybody out." Mrs. Sweet demanded

Everybody got out. Water walked over to the water fountain, grabbing him and her a cup to chill or to stay hydrated. Even though the room wasn't hot. It felt like it.

They onto us, Water. Mrs. Sweet says

Who is onto us? Asked Water

"THE FBI." Mrs. Sweet leaned over the table.

Soon it will be coast guard, searching for lives that you have killed after fucking them. It's bad enough their minors, bad enough that you were cheating on me for the last 13 years of this marriage but leaving their bodies without burning them so they can be identified inside and out. " Mrs. Sweet explained

" Why yes, you see as intelligent as you are. You would think that the crime team would have a team where they identify Burned bodies as well " Water says.

Water raises his arms.

"So what's the point of burning them where they can be identified either way? ." Water said

And yes I fucked them, and none of them girls were loose. If you know what I mean. " Water said sipping his water.

" At least your homeboy Sky can last long and shoot longer too, if you know what I mean. " Mrs. Sweet said sipping her water, staring at him as she dranked the rest of her water. Raising her plastic cup to him as a way to say thank you. Leaving the office.

Water shook his head

" I walked into that one. " Water said to himself

A worker of his ran to him.

Sir, we have an emergency." The worker said

Water ran to the emergency, seeing what was going on. The upstairs vault was stolen. The estate that they kept was gone. Water's face became red. Yelling in anger.

"HOW DID THIS HAPPEN? He asked

Show me the security cameras.

Security camera room 1 it said on the door. Slamming it.

Footage of Kena going into the vault. Mela in camera 1.

Run a face swipe.

Locating the face, they couldn't match the intruder.

Water knew better. That was Kena Peace.

The FBI walked into the bank, asking to speak to the owner.

" ALRIGHT, EVERYONE STAY CALM, PLEASE EXIT THE BUILDING. Says the captain

People ran out of the building instead of being calm.

" LET ME SPEAK TO THE OWNER. " The captain said

Water walked in the long hallway, leaning over the stairwell.

The captain gave a grin.

" YOU WATER STREET? . The Captain asked. Yelling at the top of his lungs

" WE HAVE A WARRANT." The captain said raising his eyebrows

Captain jogging up the stairs.

" SEARCH ALL HIDDEN DOCUMENTS." Says the captain

Anything that will help with this case. The captain says softly.

" Long time no see. " The captain says

Face to face they stood.

The captain walked away

" Oh, heard from your son?." The captain asked

Water takes a deep breath.

He has been kidnapped, and nobody has found him since 5 weeks ago.

About the Author

Masonia Williams goes to LA Film School. She is also an author of three books. " The Eyes of Contrnelle" and To Be You: The Beginning, along with stories everywhere on smashwords. . She currently lives Iowa with her family.